JESUS

BRIAN WILDSMITH

OXFORD
UNIVERSITY PRESS

The angel Gabriel was sent by God to a young girl called Mary who lived in Nazareth.
'God has chosen you,' said the angel. 'You will have a son and you will give him the name
Jesus. He will be called the Son of God.'

Almost nine months later, Mary and her husband Joseph had to make a long journey to
Bethlehem.

They had to sleep in a stable because there was no room for them in the inn.
And there, surrounded by animals, Mary's son was born under the light of a shining star.

Shepherds were guarding their sheep when angels appeared in the sky. They told them the good news that the Son of God had been born in Bethlehem.

The shepherds hurried to Bethlehem and found Mary and Joseph, and the baby Jesus lying in a manger.

Meanwhile three wise men from the East came to see King Herod. 'Where is the new-born King of the Jews?' they asked. 'We have seen his star rising.'

The chief priests replied, 'The prophets say he will be born in Bethlehem.'

Then Herod told the wise men: 'Go and find the child. And when you have found him, come back and tell me.'

The wise men travelled on, following the star, until it stopped above the stable where the little child had been born. They went in and opened their treasure chests and gave him presents of gold, frankincense, and myrrh.

That night an angel appeared to Joseph and said, 'Take Mary and the baby to Egypt.
Herod's soldiers are looking for Jesus. They want to kill him.' So Joseph got up at once and
escaped to Egypt.

The wise men had been warned in a dream not to go back to Herod, and they returned
to their own country by a different road.

After Herod's death, Jesus's family returned to Nazareth. When he was twelve, his parents took Jesus to the temple in Jerusalem for a festival. When it was over, Mary and Joseph set off home but didn't realize that Jesus wasn't with them. They went back and found him in the temple, asking the teachers questions. Everyone was amazed.

The years passed. A prophet, called John, told people to wash themselves in the River Jordan as a sign they wanted to lead a new life.

Jesus left his home in Nazareth and was baptized by John in the river. The spirit of God appeared like a dove, and a voice from heaven said, 'You are my dear son.'

The Devil came to tempt Jesus in the desert. 'If you're hungry', said the Devil, 'turn these stones into bread.' But Jesus refused. The Devil then took him to the roof of the temple. 'Throw yourself down. God's angels will protect you', he said. Again Jesus refused.

   He then showed Jesus all the kingdoms of the world and said, 'All this shall be yours if you worship me.' 'You should only worship God', said Jesus. And the Devil left him.

Jesus returned home and went with his mother to a wedding in Cana. The wine ran out before the party was over. 'Fill these jars with water', said Jesus. When the guests tasted it, the water had turned into very fine wine.

Later, Jesus was walking by the Sea of Galilee and saw Simon Peter and his brother Andrew fishing. 'Follow me and you will be fishers of men', said Jesus.

One day Jesus was out on Peter's fishing boat. 'Throw your net into the water', he said. 'We've fished all night and caught nothing', said Peter. But they did as Jesus had told them and the net came up full of fish.

Jesus went to a town called Nain. Near the city, bearers were carrying out a young man who had just died. He was his mother's only son, and she was a widow. Jesus said, 'Young man, rise up'. The dead man sat up and began to speak. And everyone was astonished.

Jesus then chose twelve special friends to be with him, and to help him with his work. He called them his disciples.

He sat down on the top of a hill and taught them, together with the crowds of people who had come to hear the Good News about God.

Jesus was out with his friends on a boat. He was very tired, and soon fell asleep. Suddenly a fierce storm blew up. His friends shook him awake. Jesus got up and called to the wind and the rain: 'Be still'. And there was a great calm.

They reached the other side of the lake and Jesus taught the crowds. When evening came everyone was hungry. 'We've only got five loaves and two fishes', said the disciples. 'And there are five thousand people her

'Tell them all to sit down', said Jesus. Then he took the loaves and fishes and blessed them. The disciples took the food around – and to their great surprise everyone had enough to eat. There was enough food left to fill twelve baskets.

Jesus was called to the home of a little girl. Her father, Jairus, thought she was dead. 'Little girl', said Jesus gently, 'it's time to get up'. She opened her eyes, got up, and kissed her parents.

The disciples were out on a boat one night and they saw Jesus walking towards them, on the water. Peter leapt overboard and tried to walk on the water too, but he started to sink. Jesus held out his hand. 'Have faith, Peter', he said, and saved him.

The next day he asked Peter, 'Who do you think I am?'

'You are the Christ', said Peter, 'the Son of God.'

'God has revealed this to you', said Jesus. 'You will be the leader of my church.'

A week later, Jesus took Peter, together with James and John, and led them to the top of a high mountain. Suddenly the three disciples saw Jesus change. His clothes were dazzling white, and they saw Moses and Elijah talking with him.

A voice from heaven spoke: 'This is my dear son. Listen to him.' And they were alone again on the mountain with Jesus.

Jesus received a message from two sisters, Mary and Martha: 'Our brother Lazarus is very ill'. When Jesus arrived, the sisters told him Lazarus was dead. 'Have faith', said Jesus.

Jesus told the people to take the stone away from the tomb. Then he called, 'Lazarus, come out'. And Lazarus came out, wrapped in white linen.

The next day parents brought children to Jesus. His disciples told them to go away but Jesus said, 'Let the children come to me. They belong to God's Kingdom.'

Jesus was on his way to Jerusalem and stopped in Jericho. The chief tax collector there was called Zacchaeus. He was a very small man and couldn't see Jesus because of the crowds. So he climbed a tree. Jesus looked up and said, 'Zacchaeus, come down. I'm going to stay at your house today.'

From that day on, Zacchaeus was changed. 'I will give half my money to the poor', he said.

Jesus was close to Jerusalem now. Outside the city, some friends brought him a donkey.

Jesus sat on the donkey and rode along the road to Jerusalem. There were great crowds of people standing by the road. Some had cut down branches from the palm trees and were waving them.

'Hosanna!' the people shouted. 'Hosanna! It's the man who comes from God.'

The little donkey carried Jesus through the streets of Jerusalem until they stopped in front of the temple. Jesus went inside and saw it was full of people busy buying and selling. He drove them all out, shouting, 'My house is supposed to be a house of prayer, not a den of thieves!'

This made the chief priests very angry. They thought that Jesus was a threat to them and they decided to have him killed.

For the rest of that week Jesus stayed in the city secretly, out of sight of the chief priests. On the Thursday he went to have supper with his friends, the twelve disciples.

He broke the bread and said: 'Take and eat this. It is my body.' And he lifted up the cup of wine and said: 'Take and drink this. It is my blood.'

After supper Jesus and his friends went to the garden of Gethsemane. 'Sit here and keep watch while I pray', said Jesus. But his friends fell asleep, leaving Jesus alone.

'Father', Jesus prayed, 'save me from death. But only if that is what you want.'

Three times he prayed, and three times he went back to his friends. But they were still fast asleep.

Suddenly a crowd of people came into the garden, led by Judas, one of Jesus's friends.
They seized Jesus and dragged him to the house of Caiaphas, the chief priest.

'Are you the Son of God?' Caiaphas asked.

'I am', Jesus replied.

'You have all heard these terrible words', said Caiaphas. 'What do you say?'

'He deserves to die', they cried.

The priests took Jesus to Pilate, the Roman Governor, and accused him of many things.

'Have you no answer?' said Pilate. But Jesus did not reply.

'What shall I do with him?' asked Pilate.

'Crucify him!' they all shouted.

'Take him and crucify him then,' said Pilate. 'I wash my hands of him.' So the soldiers gave Jesus a huge wooden cross and forced him to carry it.

They took Jesus to a hill outside the city.

There they crucified him between two thieves.

His friends placed the body of Jesus in a new tomb, cut out of the rock, and placed a heavy stone in front.

Early on Sunday two of Jesus's friends came. The stone had been rolled away and the body of Jesus was gone.

Two angels were there. 'He is not here,' said the angels. 'He is alive again.'

Near the tomb was a garden, and the women saw a man standing there. They thought he was the gardener, but when he turned round they knew it was Jesus.

'Don't be afraid', said Jesus. 'Run and tell all my friends to go up to Galilee, and they will see me there.'

Jesus's friends were so happy to see him again. He stayed with them for forty days, teaching them about the Kingdom of God.

But Jesus knew that it was near the time for him to leave this earth. As the sun rose one morning, he went up to his father in Heaven.

At the festival of Pentecost, the disciples were all together. Suddenly there was a sound as of a rushing wind and God's power touched them like flames of fire.

They went out into the world to tell people about Jesus and the Kingdom of God.

For Aurélie

OXFORD
UNIVERSITY PRESS

Great Clarendon Street, Oxford OX2 6DP

Oxford University Press is a department of the University of Oxford.
It furthers the University's objective of excellence in research, scholarship,
and education by publishing worldwide in

Oxford New York

Athens Auckland Bangkok Bogotá Buenos Aires Calcutta
Cape Town Chennai Dar es Salaam Delhi Florence Hong Kong Istanbul
Karachi Kuala Lumpur Madrid Melbourne Mexico City Mumbai
Nairobi Paris São Paulo Singapore Taipei Tokyo Toronto Warsaw
with associated companies in Berlin Ibadan

Oxford is a registered trade mark of Oxford University Press
in the UK and in certain other countries

British Library Cataloguing in
Publication Data available

ISBN 0 19 279059 5

Typeset by Mike Brain

Printed in Hong Kong